D is for Dump Truck

A Construction Alphabet

Written by Michael Shoulders and Illustrated by Kent Culotta

A is for Alarm

Alarm goes off. Hip-hip-hooray!
The wait is over. Today's the day.
Round up equipment and the crew.
There's construction work to do, do, do.

B is for Bulldozer

Bulldozer is tough. His work is hard.
Huffing and puffing across the yard.
Leveling land and clearing bushes.
Moving dirt, he push, push, pushes.

C is for Cut

Cut the lumber for the floors.
Plywood sheets and four-by-fours.
Sawdust on my shoes and clothes,
in my hair and nose, nose, nose.

D is for Dump Truck

Dump truck delivers a load of sand.
We need to have a lot on hand.
He backs up with a load piled deep.
Reverse horn blares out: beep, beep, beep.

E is for Eyeglasses

Eyeglasses are a construction must
to protect our eyes from flying dust.
Safety first is always key.
We need our eyes to see, see, see.

F is for Front-End Loader

Front-end loader moves a pile.
Shoveling by hand would take a while.
Lower the bucket. Come in swift.
Raise the arm up: lift, lift, lift.

G is for Grab

"Grab a hard hat," the foreman says.
"We need protection for our heads.
Falling tools leave nasty lumps."
Oops, oops! Look out!
Bump, bump, bump.

H is for Hammer

Hammer and nails, you are strong.
With you, our project won't take long.
The right tools make any work a snap.
Hold pieces together: tap, tap, tap.

tap!

I is for Imagination

Imagination is an important tool.
Dream it, draw it, and make it cool.
Gather paper, pen, and ink.
Use our brains to think, think, think.

J j

J is for Jigsaw

Jigsaw creates a nighttime scene
to put above us when we dream.
It cuts a straight or curvy line.
These stars and moon look
fine, fine, fine.

K is for Kneepads

Kneepads protect us from bumps and knocks.
On rough ground covered with stones or rocks,
building is tough on workers' knees.
If kneeling, wear them, please, please, please.

L is for Level
Levels are handy and can't be beat
for making sure steps are plumb and neat.
If the lines don't frame the bubble,
we'll have trouble, trouble, trouble.

M is for Mixer

Mixer, back up. It's your turn.
    Water, cement, spin, and churn.
       Twirl-twirl around. We need lots more.
Open your chute and pour, pour, pour.

N is for Nuts and Bolts
Nuts and bolts connect big things:
metal eye screws and tire swings.
A slide is also on the list.
Grab the wrench and twist, twist, twist.

O is for Orange Cones

Orange cones are carefully placed out on
several spots around the lawn.
They warn drivers to beware,
Mom's roses are there, there, and there.

P is for Pulley

Pulley lifts our bucket high.
Our things go upwards toward the sky:
construction tools and water jug.
Pull the rope hard: tug, tug, tug.

Q is for Quad-Axle Truck

Quad-axle trucks are ideal
    when heavy loads need extra wheels.
        Trucks sputter and strain with big cargo.
    "Ease off the gas, driver. Slow, slow, slow!"

R is for Rollers

Rollers make painting a cinch.
We need to cover every inch.
Also use a pan and brush.
Careful: do not
rush, rush, rush.

S is for Staple Gun

Staples hold things in their places:
    electrical wires or tall bookcases.
There's lots to fasten before we stop.
    Staple gun loaded: pop, pop, pop.

T is for Tape Measure

Tape measures help us pick the spot.
We must be perfect. We have one shot.
Be careful when marking. Be precise.
Measure two times then slice, slice, slice.

Tt

U is for Up

Up, up, up the rafter goes.
Set it down—right on the nose.
Careful, we're way off the ground.
Hammer it on:
pound, pound, pound.

V is for Vibrator Compactor

Vibrator compactor does the trick.
Rattle quickly; pound every brick.
It takes strong hands to operate.
Vrooom! The sidewalk is
straight, straight, straight.

W is for Wrench

Wrench turns screws to hold the wood.
 These new windows are looking good.
  The edges line up flush and tidy.
 Remember: Lefty-loosy,
          right-tight-tighty.

X is for X-Braces

X-braces help walls stand up stronger.
They will make them last much longer.
When the foreman is satisfied,
bolt the boards: side to side.

Y is for Yard

Yard clean-up time has come.
Who helps pick up? Everyone!
The job is done when the foreman has seen
the construction site is clean, clean, clean.

Y y

Z is for Zippers

Zippers close up sleeping bags.
Our eyes are droopy and start to sag.
We'll enjoy our house up in the trees.
Nighty-night! Let's catch some Zzzzs.

Construction Glossary

cargo heavy items carried from one place to another

cement material that is mixed with water to make concrete

crew the group of people who work on a construction site

equipment supplies, tools, and machinery needed for a construction project

foreman the person in charge

lumber wooden boards used to build homes and buildings

plumb to be perfectly straight

plywood a strong board made by gluing together many thin sheets of wood

rafter parallel beams that support a roof

For Jonas Jeffrey McFadden who loves construction sites

—Michael

For Patrick, my champion

—Kent

Text Copyright © 2016 Michael Shoulders
Illustration Copyright © 2016 Kent Culotta

2395 South Huron Parkway, Suite 200
Ann Arbor, MI 48104
www.sleepingbearpress.com

Printed and bound in the United States.

10 9 8 7 6 5 4 3 2 1

Library of Congress Cataloging-in-Publication Data

Names: Shoulders, Michael, author. | Culotta, Kent, illustrator.

Title: D is for dump truck : a construction alphabet / written by Michael Shoulders ; illustrated by Kent Culotta.

Description: Ann Arbor, MI : Sleeping Bear Press, [2016] | Audience: Ages 4-8.

Identifiers: LCCN 2016007651 | ISBN 9781585369751

Subjects: LCSH: Construction equipment--Juvenile literature. Construction

industry--Juvenile literature. | Alphabet--Juvenile literature. Alphabet books.

Classification: LCC TH149 .S527 2016 | DDC 629.225--dc23

LC record available at http://lccn.loc.gov/2016007651